GIRL
KING

AKRON SERIES IN POETRY

AKRON SERIES IN POETRY
Mary Biddinger, Editor

Titles published since 2008.
For a complete listing of titles published in the series,
go to www.uakron.edu/uapress/poetry.

GIRL KING

BRITTANY CAVALLARO

The University of Akron Press
Akron, Ohio

19 18 17 16 15   5 4 3 2 1

ISBN: 978-1-937378-97-4 (cloth)
ISBN: 978-1-937378-98-1 (paper)
ISBN: 978-1-937378-99-8 (ePDF)
ISBN: 978-1-629220-00-0 (ePub)

LIBRARY OF CONGRESS CATALOGING-IN-PUBLICATION DATA
Cavallaro, Brittany.
 [Poems. Selections]
Girl-king / Brittany Cavallaro.
    pages cm. — (Akron series in poetry)
ISBN 978-1-937378-97-4 (hardback) — ISBN 978-1-937378-98-1 (paper) —
ISBN 978-1-937378-99-8 (epdf)
I. Title.
PS3603.A89895A6 2015
811'.6—dc23

                    2014044270

∞ The paper used in this publication meets the minimum requirements of ANSI /
NISO Z39.48–1992 (Permanence of Paper).

Cover: *Shadow of Doubt* by Emma Bennett, © 2009, photographed by Peter Abrahams,
and reproduced with permission. Cover design by Lauren McAndrews.

Girl-King was designed and typeset in Garamond by Amy Freels and printed on sixty-
pound natural and bound by Bookmasters of Ashland, Ohio.

Contents

for my parents

The Girl in Question

What the girl goes through to get here—thickets,
coverlets, the half-built halls of this manor
and its elegant, crumbling drawbridges, the tease
of the moat beneath. She stops at its banks. Her frock
is on wrong but she can't help herself, and what's below
knows her, knows her buttoning hands. *Hello*
she says back to the water *you wouldn't let me float*
would you? but the moat would like her to unroll
the grass on the other side, to fasten it shut
like skin over a sore. She hesitates. Behind her
the chanting. She knows there is a boy in the wood
who has dropped to his knees and drawn a circle
and is saying each of her secret names. *Susanna*
he says *Silent Dog* and *White Scarf* and she tightens
hers to hear her pulse. *Mend my wrapping coat* he says
I am so cold. The water begs, the boy begs her
and she could pull a girl from the storm cellar, a twin,
tornado-legged and frozen, from her hiding-place
in the icebox, the place she learned her breath's
real shape, a twin from the shaved-grass garden.
She could teach them how to mend, to wait for the final
girl on the road, the one who will not answer.
How to wait for the answer. How to tell them apart.

Girl-King

Points of Issue

Errors or peculiarities in a book that help to differentiate it from other editions.

No one else's marginalia inside. An unbroken spine
and a pliable binding. No one else's marginalia

unless it was penciled into her first pages then
thoroughly erased. No ellipses but in the last chapters

and then only in soliloquy. No strands of hair
in the meadow chapter, nothing ripped out

in the two after that. And halfway—a blank page,
and a scrawl and dash from the girl. The final story

of the back garden and her coiled braids
and the dappled grey you kept too long.

The harmonica on the dashboard and the girl
who taught you your scales. And the book

you were always reading, the pulled-off,
pockmarked cover, the weight. The night

you left it in the truck bed and in the morning
its swollen pages. The girl reading

your father's Wordsworth, the scrolling
clouds in the meadow, your hands steady

on her heaving chest. The final story
of the back garden and the coiled girl

telling you *no.* The pages after that.

Bildungsroman

Her ripped red frock
on the wet lawn, her inside
it. She knew years had passed
since the woolly caterpillars.
Her mother's lips still the color
of the yew berries that could not
be eaten in threes & then there
was the boy who wanted if only
she missed with her cherry
bombs. She went to the copse
behind her house, it had arms.
She was her dress. And then
there was the dog & the dog
understood. He hated the bow
holding his neck together, he knew
the clawed halls of her own. So
he fed her crabapples, mashed
them soft with his mouth & when
she could talk again he doctored
her with the under-sink chemicals,
nosed the cabinet door open—
she happily sucked their nozzles,
pumped their levers, she gained
strength, her mouth opened
& closed now, if slowly. He took
her to the party with the polio
children, she daintily licked each
of their half-eaten cakes when
proffered by his black paw. Then

her arms! She shoved her stuffed
animals against the wall
& demanded alibis, the dog said
for their own sakes, he slammed
his head's black gavel against hers
& declared everyone innocent
of every crime. She was overcome.
The dog crawled under the porch
& she dragged her small body
along. She mulched herself in
with the dog gone flimsy & wet,
she ate from his warm belly to help
with the growing. She grew.

Magician's Girl

You'll know when. My gossamer singlet flushes
        to its ends in fire. The black hats, too, begin
            to hate you. One wrong word & their brims curl

to reveal knives. By Thursday, the floor translates

your foot-falls as Morse code. At your step,
        the oubliette opens. Another narrow not-death
            & the curtains become girls again. They leave

you again. They don't love you like Mother does,

bound to the velvet board, febrile Mother willing
        your water-tank, your white-gloved touch,
            the part of her night where she is finally a half

of you. Despite the involvement of blades. Despite

my holding-down hands. She knows
        about your knob-kneed bedmates, their soft
            white hair. Girls lost in the long warren

of your arms. Big-toothed girls, girls who disappear

& disappear. You blame yourself. Why? You
        don't know that what you do in the dark
            of your room—I do it too? Watch closely. Here

are my man's hands. Here is my girl's mouth, speaking—

Lies I Told

I never made my living
on the phone. I didn't see you,
I'm sorry. Maybe the cold
rain, or the nighttime. Anyway,
gin is my favorite. Your house
is fine; I always walk two miles
to work and I'd love to see
your succulents. Of course
I never wore your Arran sweater
while I stirred the red sauce. I always
washed my hands. I washed
my sheets, between, and when
they were red, I'd made it up
that morning. When I laid late
in bed, I was reading, the book
of course Russian. I wore the lace,
the piece you talk about. I didn't
tear it on purpose. Your dog
seemed to like the hot backseat,
lying in the sun that way
like a lover. I never loved anyone
before I loved you. The far end
is the shallow one, I promise,
I came here as a child.
I'll never need another father.
I clapped for you, afterward,
but the banquet hall was so familiar
and you were so familiar, up there,
and I was so happy.

Postcard from Perugia, Post-Wedding

I told my mother everything
I'd had. About the ashes.

About the last hotel. The towels
suspended from their bars, black-

streaked from my eyes. The flies
that follow us, waiting. Balconies

where he hangs to test his grip. For
me. My swallowed key. Beloved

throwing a blow-out sale before
closing. Those of us surviving on

just one name. The last time I put
my own to paper. If elopement

implies bride as white rabbit, these streets
teem with top hats. But she knows

all this. I was born here, you know.

The Virgin Disambiguates

Today, a test to identify my bones, the door
to your room swung shut. Don't say
anything with your mouth. Try this: before

words, a lettered spine, one language ancient, more
aware than you of what *body* means. Today
a mouse, unboned, blacked like rot beneath our door,

a dirty coin. You argue like a Tudor
scholar—for the right to touch, you play
upon *compliant* and *complaint*. Before

you ask, Marvell's mistress sent no letters, pored
instead over her own anatomy. O gray
mouse, I disjoint. My body, a dark fillet under your door.

Bone saws can't cut through tongue. Ignore
this blinding white of alphabet, letters on my slate-
cold body, my mouth a harmless cocktail. *Bar the door,
Maria*, this door of new-grown bones.

Superstition

All the children are swimming in wells
and they are not drowning. Quick pull up the buckets.

I dowse with my two-pronged stick,
find duck teeth, tiger eggs, smooth whole hearts.

The clouds move like scissors subtracting sky.
In the attic I shear my wedding dress to my knees.

I repeat your name until I forget mine,
push my hands through the mirror at midnight.

And Brittany—you are no magician's girl so why
do you let him saw through all your articulate ribs.

White-Armed Persephone Walks into His Van

She stripped wisteria off the pronged
poles. Wednesday. The mistake garden
           plot by the Stop-n-Shop on Grand

      where they wait. Pumping premium into her
pickup, she decides to yes the next man
           who asks. Her knees

      above her knee socks guarantee. Her
riding skirt rising as she reaches for
           flowers to dress her mother's table. When

      her daughter is an open feast. When
she leans to squeegee her windshield
           and the tattooed man reaches out then

      under. His white van idles louder. When
the bird-whistles across the highway
           open her in her car. The pistils

in her glove. She always knew she'd go
           quietly. The hidden knives agree.

Aperture

Good. You, consummate
professional—cold-stripped

field, requisite white dress.
The finished editorial

will be titled *End* as it is
night & we are sure

someone can be held
responsible. The clean man

moves your limbs like a stop-
motion film. I stick the cake

with fetching sparklers. There is
a flurried debate about you

in fur, as you will be under
the train. We are kind. We talk

to you about flowering
as if you could, in fact, open.

Do you know you haven't bled
yet? Your mother says not

to worry, you have a whole
life to. You won't. We shoot—

Girl-King

The girl stays low in the rushes. She eyes her throne through
her lashes. The Twelfth-cake found her with its queening clutch
of peas and after dispatching the bean king (like an axe
from its handle) she began her ascension. Like the axe
handed to her by her mother when they lived
in the burnt-out tree, her limbs folded into clothing,
her feet arranged on the road—she is the crime,
her mother made her so. An arm pigeon-slinged
and blooded, the black dog panting beside her. And the man
in the first house and the serving trays and the scullery nights
she wears like a black birthmark, all that beating
in her chest. And now the twelfth night. And the woman
picking her teeth with a crow bone, the woman
whip-cord thin. And the girl underneath her chair, her hatchet.

Eliza-Crossing-the-Ice

Saturday matinee. Today she's lashed
to the tracks. Because she ran off
with the mustached man. The girl watches
him labor over her body, and she does not
think about the train. The thick rope
is so beautiful. She is bound and full
as a hope chest. Inside, the pies
she made from the birds he'd shot,
her white ice skates, the line she dropped
from her window. The line that ties her
now, back to her mother and to the quiet
books, the belladonna pressings
in their leaves, dried larkspur from
the cellar ceiling. Her mother's hands
pressing her gently to the ground,
the tight bows tied. No cursive narration.
And he's tried to unbind her, but the day's
grown cold, his fingers, cold, and the sound
louder down the line. It isn't until he mounts
his horse that she starts to yell through
the bloody rag.

       In the theater, the piano man
plays an explanation. There's a house on fire,
a bordello girl, there are gold-rush prospects.
She's a low-hanging peach. She's never seen
the lake in winter. She's never skated out
a figure-eight while someone watched
for her to fall. But she's down, and the train
comes, and the music stiffens. Quiet now.

Twins

On the hazel there are nuts to be enjoyed,
but the ash never bears fruit.
"Le Fresne," Marie de France

Because you know if I say
mother. Say I will follow
him through the dark fields.
The limbs a spray of dry-
mouthed grey. His horse
stuttering on the path. Say

mother, I am not the last
one. Two girls in your womb
meant two men's sweat
in your bed. So. You hid

me in the ash tree. Gave
my other a name. *Le Codre—*
no present. Instead a shade
of hay she won't be rolled

in. Fruit-fat she keeps
her tokens, keeps her men
hungry. Her doubtless coin
doubling in her belly. Mother,

when he finds me curled
like some last smoke, bed-
bleeding again, *je veux dire*
tu veux me voir. I'll give myself

then. In the night. I will lay
my dress on the bed to bless
them. An expanse of girls
expanding still & I, a cast off
rind of her, writhing. The tree
split open by the spring.

Adulteress

The dark, indelicate question of *who*.
The skin of her face clutched up
like a sailor's knot. Wants other arms.
Will wrap them around her neck,
wait for the tendons to contract.
Wants the roving eye to stop on her,
a searchlight. Then the black garden.
Then the coins. She asks herself & so
replies. She plants her face knowing it
will clutch upward into a calyx. She casts
herself in mold & her double in the back
garden, warning. In the southern town
the pay phone again, a gurgled sea. A string
of songbirds from the washing line.
The *chanson* that told girl-her how to work on
herself. Body. Where there is someone.
Someone with legs and teeth and hair
not the concavities without. *Alouette,*
tu es un torse saignant. In the dream
the trees are stalactites. In the damp earth.
There is fire to hollow the trees.
The sextons are asleep so she is locating
the next resting place. The skylark
without head, wings, heart, beak.
There were bridges over the river
but the clouds ate & ate, they loll now
satiated, threaten with their heft.
If one stays, the others can blow
seaward. If one stays like a crumpled

incantation above the heads, those
that wanted so badly, that blew with
their hands through the bulk of her
clothes, if she could just the torso
bleeding with *yes, yes, yes, I will love you
all,* will clutch out herself and rain
more of she from above, then alone
she could make her own lake
in time for the slowest drowning.

Poem with First Two Lines from Paracelsus

All things are poison and nothing is without poison.
Only the dose makes it not poison. And the moon

was the bare bulb in the surgery. I taught myself
my lines—*redress,* and *tailor,* and *fuck*. You, the needle

dipped in blood sewing me together. I hid the pills
in a hollow tooth. An in or an out. No one believed me

in this role—pupils blown out, begging for love.
Or I wait up til three but you're still married. I wait up

another year, then I am too. It's a shell game,
shuffling the years, looking for the empty fist

or the vial filled with water. We change the dates
to make it work. We pay ourselves back. What we did

in the sound booth? I cut the stitches to find the light
underneath. Then I wore your coat home. At the party

we behaved. The windows wore their shades
like a row of winking eyes. I washed off your smell

in the claw-foot because I knew you'd enter anyway.
Intermission: when you bit through the sheet to stay silent,

I pushed myself down, mouthing *I love you, I love you.*
It wasn't allowed in corsets. It wasn't allowed

by the creek in the copse. I fixed us old fashioneds
in disallowed braids. I wore red desperation to the bar,

drank digitalis, sugared almonds for your tea. I bit through
my own stitches. I sent you back to your wife. I didn't care,

because I couldn't, and so I broke open each molar
with a hammer. I didn't care, and so on the long flight home

I let the blood string down my chin in lashes. I let
the others cover their eyes the way I should have done.

Transmigration

Knowing the hound is worth
a hundred days of foxes. Knowing
the huntsmen by name & the shape
they take at supper. Knowing her daughter
the mother collared her into a cloak
& loosed her in the wood. The girl
returned as a red deer,
as a flock of swans & once
she was a kennel. Her belly took in
litters, she collapsed only when run over
by the horse-mad men. Even then
game came home in her many mouths.
And then the day she was found in
the neighbor's stables, her new-grown hands
held up to stop the hooves. Dirty-faced
at table, her mother taught her to pull apart
her fingers. She was nine. The next time she fled
she became the holes in the vegetable garden,
rabbits squirmed in those tight snares. How
was not asked. The family was fed. Men
stopped by the house to ask for the cast-off
dresses, for the bits of girl-skin in her bed
sheets, tokens to take on their hunt. None
were given, so the men caught nothing.
Her garden throats howled & the white foxes
heard, they hid in her dirt. The men
dug her up, they were starving.
She was taken home to bed. Her mother
remembered the nights she too had spent

head-down in the ground. She knew
the deep places & was done. How her own shape
formed like apples then fell
into gathering hands. Her own daughter now
the best trap. Her daughter, the fowl
in her teeth, the trail of bones behind her.

The Resurrectionists

Up the close and down the stair,
No one is safe from Burke and Hare.
Burke's the butcher, Hare's the thief,
Knox, the one who buys the beef.
—Scottish skipping rhyme, nineteenth century

"Notwithstanding the extreme views the people of Scotland held against the resurrectionists, as the body snatchers were named, their horrible trade continued to prosper and it received many recruits. The surgeons even gradually dropped into the business, perhaps not themselves engaging in it personally but at least sanctioning and approving of it by the purchase of the bodies offered them. But besides these a class of men became resurrectionists as a matter of trade and no churchyard in the country was safe from their depredations."
—*The History of Burke and Hare and The Resurrectionist Times*, 1884

J. J. Audubon on His Stay in Edinburgh

Noctuary: The suitcase safekeeping my sketches.
No dining with Walter Scott tonight. He hides
with his novel and his life
of Napoleon but *I shall see him if I have to crawl
on all fours for a mile*. In the Grassmarket

two corvid girls outside the White Hart trembling.
I buy their flowers. I buy the baskets
for the flowers, they are things
that will be beautiful
when drawn. Noctuary: The Scottish ornithologists

tell me of the one-eyed Robert Knox who may want
to see my American birds. Noctuary: The louche city
prone in the rain. Took sketches to Knox,
this night his only opening, him sweeping out
in an over-gown

and with bloody fingers. He tells me his Anatomy School
is allotted one corpse each year, a man condemned
to death then dissection. Ten corpses
tonight waited like women at supper. Where
from? Noctuary: The song
they sing in the Grassmarket: Knox is *the boy*

who buys the beef. Knox buys the veal
as well. At the School, one of those filthy girls
on the table, smothered—this was disagreeable.
Glad to leave this charnel house. Glad to have my flowers
in my homebound bag.

Girl 2

Father there is no parchment at the end of this hallway

Father I am using my open throat to tell you

Father the last one I opened I didn't rescind the invitation

Father he cowers in the eaves it's your pillowy light

Father gave me legs so I could split four ways

Father in the crouched room at the church-back

Father in what he held under his chin

Father in the nails keeping on his shoes

Father

Father

Father this is my home now

Father I've waited

Robert Knox, To a Supplier

In the French method I teach them one
to a cadaver, as if all are equal—what cold, stiff things
allowed on the black marble, their ends that curl

like the ends of lilies, what upright men
before them. Indeed, when you write my hagiography
I would take my own works on Cuvier

and Saint-Hilare (those artist-anatomists) as examples
of how I should be laid out. I knot the strings
between the men and their bodies, between the box

and the well-lit room. I was schooled in Paris and I lunch
on Charlotte Square and you, my friend,
are a fool. You threaten me with a shovel? When I go

into the ground, I will never come back.

William Burke in the Tanner's Close Lodging-House

"Burke and Hare took for their motto the significant question Burke put to the student when he was negotiating for the sale of [their first] body: 'Wouldn't you give a pound more for a fresh one?'"

After we fill his coffin with bark and bury it we will bring Knox the corpse. We are not doctors but Hare is sure there is an abscess in his mouth for it is thrown open like a door and inside the red parts are still wet like there is a working tongue. At night I am sure it roves the room tasting. I am in my bed and the boardinghouse shudders like it is stroked down by a heavy hand. I can sleep. Knox will pay more for the body. It is diseased and he studies the unsecured. Hare is sure there is a light in the house across the street and his Margaret too agrees. Margaret has abscesses even my untrained eye can see. The light it goes red and I pull the pillow over my head and through it my breathing labors. How I want it to. Hare is sure of it. There is a way to take a body whole in the night.

Girl 3

After the sale of their first body, a tenant of Margaret's who died in the night, Burke and Hare began smothering women and tramps they lured in from the street with the assistance of Margaret and Burke's lover Helen.

He swept out my hair with the straw

and his young friend sang 'while with thee

on grassy pillow solitude I love to dwell'

it kept me still his long body laid over mine

and the other held it above me held it

there was a gold shilling for every minute

I had been buried with them no one

would know when Knox started his knives

on my face Burke and Hare had my hands

Margaret Hare, To a Tenant

When my Logue
was dead and buried I chose the top-
floor lodger to keep an eye on mine. My William Hare
was an ugly man and uglier still his teeth,

his whiskey-stumble laugh (laughing
he looked as though he'd been taught each one
of his sorry years, laughed when Burke hit him

and when Burke shook the deal table and when Burke
handled his whore Helen in the hall) but that tenant died
and owed three months' so the men (our men)

they dealt with it. (My sister out in Leith
she'll hear of this and know our father right.)
They took more. The sick. I took for my fee

one piece for the use of my rooms
and when I knelt at night I only prayed
for myself, Hare couldn't speak for laughing.

Mary Paterson's Daughter

*"… the girl's hair was in curl papers so that all the external
appearances were that the body was fresh and had not been
buried. Her handsome figure and well-shaped limbs so
attracted the attention of Dr. Knox that he preserved the
body for three months in spirits and invited a painter to see it."*

My mother's wigs were gifted her she dressed
in the bright colors the gentlemen liked their meat

served with mint and my mother folded bits
in a napkin for my night meal I was proud of

her restraint and her white neck she drank
at the Hart I warned her in before sundown but ladies

took visitors' cards in the day their men idle
my mother in a thick cloud of violet my mother

not breathing the students knew her had her
on their tables too her name was known the other women

were not Knox's doorman bought a sketch of her
body was *a fine specimen of a woman* I couldn't help

how proud I was

Helen McDougal, To a Runaway

Who I belong to is no matter
of yours, I reckon. You're not here
to be sought out by anyone
who might take you home.
This is where they find themselves,
that pretty sort of flower that gets
trod on in the stable but finds
in a house such as this, there's dirt
no one will try to take from
your hands. When I was left
I left the next one, left our children,
sold our clothes and their small shoes.
Last Hogmanay I heard the girl
gave herself away, the little
fool. Her trousseau all pine
and ash. There's no sun here
either but my lover knows
a song he'll teach you in
his pretty Irish voice. When he
confesses the priest feels no need
to give him absolution. My God
if you wouldn't shake like that
I'd pour you another. Child
you lie on that table as if
you've pinned yourself to it.

Girl 7

I watched them build the towers

at St. Cuthbert's at the feet of Lothian

road at the feet of the men who kneeled

in their own turn it was mine I escaped

the cold to lay in the close to lay my father

sent me to the mother house I kept my own

on beads in my pocket I wanted it in

the dark slip of the Cowgate I wanted

their hands on Palm Sunday the fronds

were rare and I didn't know who to ask

to build my tower I gave myself freely to God

I took whatever was given in return

William Burke at His Dissection

"Burke, in jail, was put up for execution. [His body] was placed naked on a black marble table in the anatomical theatre and a through passage was arranged for the accommodation of the visitors."

An old woman came to the house
as a lodger and that night I had been
singing for the men together walked
back to their houses and they were quiet
and the men together closed their doors
at dark and what they saw in the aurora
borealis was red and told stories of what
Hare and I had not yet done and I oh
my girl was no cobbler *and she was the worse*
of drink and the shoes I took from their feet
were in the torn mattress and I slept there no
my girl and Margaret could ask them to the stable
and she got more drink of her own accord and what
I asked of them I asked with this tongue Knox
took me from a boy to another boy and
he could not keep an empty table this bed
she became very drunk and declarant made
my confessions forgive me *suffocated her*
and Hare was not the one who asked me here
he hangs open his skull they say like a woman's
not a murderer's *in the house at the time*
she was disposed of in the same manner

Robert Knox, To a Girl in Labor

Rumor has Knox spending his final days as a
cheap obstetrician in London.

My dear father was a natural
philosopher and in his soft man's hands
I learned my particular language.
What autodidact did not? He taught me

to keep a good table and indeed I do keep
the flesh available for other flesh as
the blood beneath is related. My darling girl
push your child into my keeping.

Before Burke and Hare I taught myself
to keep my fingers clean. Lass,
infection is no matter; I see a boy's skull now
and its emollient cover

and you are no nullipara
once you have made yourself a man.
To think that delivery is my business as
I once was the receiver

and men clipped their ribs open
for me to wash them out.
Or some clipped—cool your sweet
head, girl, who taught you how to speak?

Mirror Songs

>   … others gave up;
> good girls gave in;
> geography was hard on friendship, Sire;
> marriages lashed & languished, anguished; dearth of group
> and what else had been;
>
> the splendour & the lose grew all the same.
> —John Berryman, "Dream Song 58"

Could Not Make Good

The rock arches, the knell of the water. She maybe
never told you: begin as ash, as a letter from
the war censored by love.
There once stood up a silence from her chest
and now she sleeps heavy. What she knew of
all she could repair? It ends, the carillon.

Of the thousand things she keeps in her file
the painting in its dark tatters
is spotlit and so laughs. Her flushed face
always before it. That is her response
to its sharp edges, the shaking in the water,
the foam of her night-cry.

And of the whole bodies, what walked back out
up the mountain, still drenched
in their ridicule? She doesn't think. In the night
she steps around them in the hall.
They will all leave for the ocean again.
There are not enough hands to count the missing.

Your Shotgun

My father has my feathers. All girls, wasp-
waisted and veined like thirsty leaves, touch
and touch their edges.
They are meant to, I know, they feel
soapy-new, they feel ill but clean, more
they ask, pile them on like teacakes.

After—O friends, keep what you've forgotten,
the whimper-light of evening on the mountains and nothing—
girls, it's your story,
swallowed for this moment, healed
like what—so grow up. Feathers like cream
when you're in the big way.

I'll tell you the lie. In the thick
of the kind & buoying gossip I gave all—
on the ship, healed—
louder—I am licked bright, in my body
my daughter will go elsewhere—I say *yes*,
knowing the girls go another way.

In Us We Trust

Sky clouds at noon, Oconomowoc storms rage
as the land discharges the peaceful
like a jack-knifing car. More, now, more ravines,
more river-basins, at the lowest point
they are on guard. Distrustful underneath
even their stone houses,

those we don't want. Sundance and pause,
rain and fall, these days we pray
for all to burn out, shine
while they do. Years from now on holiday
the tar pits uneven and insistent
as an attraction.

At this moment, the air breathes them
like lung-coal, and they stand leagues beneath
and they keen. There is no war
and so there are no stars, there is
the reeling notion
that now they are worse than dead.

Linked to the Land at Low Tide

She, unsure, skittered to the middle to take
back her stories. This future, she said, is a bar
and now is a bar too.
She rummaged through the crowd
for the broken. Girl, one said, be upset,
all you make are decisions. Hand down

the inappropriate punishment. Loosen
your short limbs, try to take up
some space. Too many directions, she said,
I'll regain my sight. At the top of this borrowed
book heap—*indication*—I am your queen.
One said, you clearly aren't.

But she remembered. She was here again.
In her waking moments she thought
of a paged ship, teeming with mice
that discarded their swords
and only slept. They are in the middle too. Here is
your map. One said, thanks for nothing.

The Knack of Ruin

She blinked at love; love had something in its eye.
She knew they were strangers. She, numb, on the street,
where his father found them, still clothed—
they were stranger, then. When every diary was found
with pages blank, she thought she'd never learn
to look straight back. They missed each other,

or missed on a steamliner; in a basement dungeon;
and over her own hand-bound journal they looked away;
and in dusky Naperville,
armed with compass & bright-eyed in the morning & earlier,
and whispering back to the letter's promise,
or when some academic asked for her hands

to hear the truth of it, 'narcoleptic.'
But she tried to forget it, that they were estranged.
She knew it all the same.
Each one was a confidant, come in with saber bright
to find the original copy, and to slide it apart.
She shook her head, re-.

The Name of This Was Freedom

Soft-lipped and bright-clawed slept not the girl on.
Soft though under her vanity blurred a mirror
peripherally, stuck there
while she was shying away from nightclubs
and forgetting.
She opened an eye, allowed it a smile.

Together. They all clustered her—forget! none,
when only she—over the moon.
It was never right.
She can work better with the mirror here, remember.
Whole, and mauve like salvation.
Secretly, this was an incarceration.

Will she again never be hiding from men & honey,
vagrancy & lust again,
have 401(k)s, Visa cards?
She didn't want to whimper but wavered as
(winter blow, bitter, sleet) two fistfuls of shout
appeared & then all slunk away.

City Where No One Is From

At the Illinois State Fair

Pray for blackouts. For
a packed grandstand. Pray for
ex-cons and no back door.
Pray for Milwaukee men eating
turkey legs whole, who watch ours
as we climb the chairlift stairs—
pray for the heavy Clydesdale
hooves and the girl who waves
the 4-H flag. For our footsteps
swept out with the dirt. We'll spike
our shake-ups and drink them
with the safety men. I'll sever
the Spider's arms so they'll fall
around its trunk; you'll watch closely
on the ground. They know we'll ride
the Himalaya, so pray for the wrong
direction. For broken levers. For
the Alabama man to drop down
onto the console. We'll clutch our
slutty drinks. We'll stumble
to the Log Jam. Pray for frayed
seatbelts. Pray for the long drop.
Pray that tonight, when our mothers
rise from their incense blankets,
their sacrificial wine, from their shrines
winking like fairway lights, when
they look down at our waiting beds—
pray for the salt in the sheets,
for the body hollows. Pray for
their mouths, then. Pray then
for the final break.

Mythomania

I met them by the silo outside
Joy Prairie. They'd called the mall

pay phone until someone picked
up. I always picked up. I was

Orange Julius forever then I was
blackest coffee. I brought them

saltwater taffy to chew on
while they looked me over.

They palmed their smokes
with a practiced hand. I asked

for consent and I shucked down
my dress and after their applause

I let them see my State Fair heart.
We went to the hot dog parking lot.

They taught me to drive their Toyotas.
They were my first time. There were

others later. Other tablecloths on
tables. Another radio. Men who

would dive down through grain
to retrieve things I'd thrown

in. Who wanted a Midwest map.
Asked *what did they do to you*

back then I always said
everything.

Mesocyclone

When I am not watching the sky,
      I am doing nothing else. June

           in Illinois, & the television tells us to stay

inside. The crows cluster on our old car
      like shavings from a scratch-off ticket

           & when the windfall comes, it brings down

our ceilings. A peeling whine, & our house
      unhouses itself. Tonight—nothing

           standing. My body first his, then yours.

The endless iterations. On the snake-hills of
      Cahokia. At the drop in Starved Rock.

           On the skyscraper's top floor & in the final

basement. We are there. Again. The funnel
      cloud fisting down; the siren baying

           a promise; the end of the twister, its silent

oh. A naught repeating. You throw our
      luggage in the car; the engine turns over

           like a man in his sleep. A girl stock-still

in the door. The crows scatter
    like tea leaves. I love you.

        Again. I love you. Now leave.

Any Ordinary Hell

The lucky girls do not have to remember
their bodies. They walk to the open-air market

each morning to buy a croissant and the *Times*.
In the newspaper they read about women sent

like brown paper packages to a civilized country
to lay down in grease and men's spit, their legs

propped open. There is a menu of services.
They are tattooed with what they owe. The lucky girls

are all reading *Jane Eyre*. They watch expensive cable
to see women in togas learn how to fuck. It is

another century. The starlet's heavy breasts heave up
against her chin so that she throws her head back

in pleasure. In Spain, a woman in red pleather boots
leans into a car. The lucky girls clutch their maps, pretty

as painted sugar bowls. They murmur, *where do we go after this.*

Autotheism

I'm sixteen. Every fact I know is filed away
in my mind palace, with its million rooms
and the lighting of a county morgue. Ask me

the slowest way to drown or how best
to remove an eye, and I will let you
sit close enough to listen. Clorox

cleans. The galaxy expands. The girl
who fidgets through my favorite class
bleeds down her seat. I count the minutes

(nine), divide by reaction (none). Still
she's invited to the party that Saturday.
I open my head like the man-god

birthing Athena but no parties will have me,
not while I know everything. The man who will
is half again me—height, mass, depth—

and lives in a loft in the meatpacking district
because he is an inventor. I tell him
once I ate a wasps' nest like it was paper

to become their benevolent god. He makes
milk cartons, he says, the light goes on
when the milk goes wrong, and then

he puts on a German film and fucks me
instead of taking me home. In my mind palace
my gait is as smooth as Lady Godiva

(tenth century, Godgift). I think of telegraphs
(1836), I beat one hand on the wood floor
like the angels are interested in a machine

like me. But the key isn't in my pockets.
He took enough of my hair to stuff a pillow
but it is not me if it can be taken away. I forgive

many things in others, nothing in myself.

A Taxonomy of Sex

Chart your own arrangement. As in: the star's heat
looped into the black hole and looped again,
this time digital, the thrust of its run pre-Coliseum,

pre-violin. Rest it in the specimen jar between
the whalebone corset and both his rough hands,
between Fialta and your Fiat's backseat, between

Nabokov and every dumb-sounding twenty-something
in heart-shaped glasses. Between your social breast
photos, your game tagged and arranged from biggest

to angriest or most likely to contradict your father
over golf. Between white sheet and ripped sheet
and bloodied hung out the window as proof. Between

alive and will stay that way. Between each dying star
an emptiness that collapses, and it happens every collapse,
the Romans kill for it, the lover lifts a single finger.

At Seventeen,

the purity ring I ate in a cake at Christmas—
your beautiful mother serving the housekeeper supper,
my knee socks puddled around my ankles, the bluff
in Marin & its army bunkers, the seven-minute traffic light,
the redingote of your palms on my new breasts, your brother
& all the requisite Neruda, hand-holding, silk scarves, leather
gloves, charity dinners in Monterey, your oil baron
uncle & all the drill bits that were never installed
except by those two hands—the San Francisco sushi bar
where I slow-pressed spines into my tongue, your dirty fingers,
my junior prom, your first premiere, the girl we sang to
on the table, the girl you'd fucked inside the playhouse,
monument, waterfall room, the sheepskin, the nights
I'd pray to my own stomach, the nights I'd pray for you
to rot, the single room, endless stream of ten-dollar words, the hangers-
on, the gut-suck & split legs, barbed wire, the thick, tin-sweet blood
that I wrung from my body into the waiting ground.

Rebellion

Back then it was always April. I stayed at the convent school
                rather than open my mouth. Because fear
    was an assignment, I excelled. I made flowcharts:

      myself to the funnel cloud. Myself to the window-well.
I curled my hair with a heated knife, and it looked
      just the same. Myself to the sinkhole where I kept

my desire. Because the black skirts considered me bright, I was left
                to my own devices. The lot the next block over,
    stocked with straight porn and dull knives

      and butt-ends: I never saw anyone there. It could exist
despite me. I liked that. The titles of black metal songs,
           the thought of salted licorice. Cherries dangled

from my rearview mirror, and that black car always
           idling outside on Wednesday nights—I called
    my friends to come, then sent them home. It was brave

      to say *yes*. I learned how to do it. I waited to be found
crying, arranged on the ground or the stairs of the theater,
           then I stood at the first hint of footsteps. Years later

when I turned off everything that wasn't me, I knew
           my wants were real but that nothing else
    was. Had never been. I knew I looked just like that actress.

Liebestod

We're all meant to go like this, in a tapestried room,
the chandelier tinkling like an insistent fork against
its oyster. We pry at the walls, find the softest part. When
the arras shifts, we see a pair of sconces, one crumpled

like the fine cloth of the man's face. She's even thinner
than in her dress, that white rag on the floor, and her hands
bite his neck the way children do. The alcove hovers over
like the Virgin. *Helen* he says *we'll be together* and slips

his smallest finger into her mouth. He could be buried
wearing her. *My love* she says *it won't hurt much longer*. The neck
is a stalk to a beautiful flower, and the last time she pulled
until she heard his collarbone crack, it rolled

back his eyes, showed the whole of their lily-
whites. That last time, it was play. He wanted to hold her
as she rattled down the dark hill to that well, to pound
those stones, to shout his name and hear only her name

echo back. It took no convincing. He wanted entry, and she
a skeleton key. *Helen* she said. He laid her on the goats-head rug
so she could count its cold teeth. There was the crowbar
and the pillow and the buckets and the sheets,

all the white sheets he could find. There was the blood,
and the next night, there was more.

Other Fields

where we wouldn't worry our mouths on
            another. There, no need to
nuzzle our heads

            into other chests, cattle-sweet. You'd make
excellent stock, I'd say now
            boiling the water—

instead we give grain in low troughs. Instead
            we touch a loved skull not
weighing or aging,

            we feel for hollows we couldn't
fill. Like the meadow trees, their knot-
            eyes sad as bullets,

like our lips concealing the original wound.
            We low—this is the open
ache. Wholly, you say,

            & here.

Dream Park

The summer after it emptied out, the dream park stayed
lofted like a kite and the city's breath kept it
there.
From each post the strings fell down

and curled and when one blew through
the window-mouth I was awake.
I tied two to the wrists my lost girl said were scissors,

I was lovely that way. My bright wrists, the party laugh

like spoon lures or spinnerbait, and though now I kept
my lips closed the sound started in my lungs.
Here is
a translucent line looped in the carpet. Here is

the one who sees it and darts away. Every morning
the dream park falls and she hoists it
up again. The strings are mine. Here and there

are scales for weighing. A sodden skirt on one side,

a raised hand on the other. The dream park
or your childhood home, bristled pink as
hidden flesh.
The summer after it emptied out, I planned

my appearance. The long linen table, my lost girl
                    strung on a necklace so I could give her away
like beads. I could pare her out of me

        like a dinner. No one said that if I pulled her in
                I'd have to toss her back.

Censored History

How beautiful, the bowl of white soup, its ginger-flesh
        garnish, the shelves of unread books re-covered
    in white wrappers. And the white dress

    on its hanger, unworn, and the password she never said
aloud after the two of you whispered it together.
        The peephole, when she peered, became

    a backwards glass, so she saw herself pinked from a bath,
cocooned in steam. Her own hair looks lanker
    than the translucent wig she wore when you met.

What hips that girl has, the bones bent forward like hands
        offering a tray. You could fold her like a napkin,
    say, look at how she rests on your lap—

    look at the round curve of her in repose, a peeled coconut,
a lacquered spoon, the jaw you can touch knowing the bone
        is as white as the skin. Lover that bathes over

    a filter then burns the paper. Her last two years
in the ash-dark soap dish. When you come back
    (you will) you'll never see what wasn't there.

Cause/Effect

Before thought,
unthought. Before silence,

a jackdaw. Where were we last?
In the morning the mouths of animals.

The stripped sky at dawn.
Before the telephone,

wings. Before ghosts, kindling.
Your expiring mouth.

Tonight the trees move
as if conveyed. The birds burrow,

burrow. The years grow lidded eyes.
Before your questioning,

knowledge. By knowledge
I mean familiarity. By questioning

I mean you dug for my bones.

Loup de Guerre

What will collapse, has,
and in the after-cough and sway,
the girl is still sleeping and her treehouse
is the bed beneath her. In the morning
she wrenches off the door and in
her hands it's a battering ram.
The bandits bring their horses by,
she is the only girl for miles. She is useful
in that general way. Over a cooking fire
they turn their spit and the girl dances
for her meal. The ram is her partner,
it sways like it has hips. There must be
some purpose here. The bandits hand her
a plate and then they fold down like a book,
the campfire, like a book, one for children.
But the ram remains, its carved head
grinning. The girl asks it to be a door
again, one that is an entrance instead of
a tearing away. The birches fold down
then, and the man comes in to ask
about his battering ram. Is it ready yet.
If she calls her mother, there will be
a departure. The long ribbons
of her heart will be taken back
and used for reins. And of course
her mother won't answer, and the ram
is still a ram. When the man folds down,
a house stands up, and through
its window she sees a crowd of women

waiting in thick station steam. Their hats
protect their eyes from the arrival. There is
a train coming. The ram edges closer
and begins its heavy lean.

Electricity, 1876

When I came to, in that year
        of bamboo, then carbon, then
                filament, I learned to make

    my own light. At night, my breasts were incandescent,

soft as white spotlighted jades.
        And the schoolgirls who knew
                how to see in the dark brought me

    back in their arms. We set up our atelier in the city's

reddest section. We plied the marquee
        makers with our sugared tips, took
                their likenesses with powdered flash;

    some took their last names. I just held their trembling faces.

When the men changed, grew
        more famous still, we painted our faces
                in an electric gold the blind could see.

    And Tesla hung our brothel lights, made our copper eggs

stand on their ends—but I took Edison
        to my bed. For him, I coiled a wet-
                licked curl and buried it in a bulb,

    I pressed my hands together. The city smoldered, then burned.

Girl-King

City where no one is from, city
that billows like the tumescent
moon, city that closes down
when the girl arrives with her bags
and her ragged diadem and all
her men. She announces herself
to the deciding park and the main gates
close. She shows her mother's brooch
and the main gates close, they cry
and they close, they've rusted. She isn't
the first. Her men attend,
they paint themselves & they press
those paintings on her, their books
explain the beginning, those waves.
The structures that wavered when
the moon came down. She has no
new reasons to send them away
& the city is hers, it wears her name
underneath, always, it won't protest—
she is terrible in her rule.

Notes

Girl-King (i): In medieval England, during the Twelfth Night festival (which ended on All Hallows Eve), a Lord of Misrule was elected during a feast. Whoever found a bean baked into his cake would be this "king" until midnight; whoever found a pea would be his queen.

Eliza-Crossing-the-Ice: Here, the title refers to the music played by a pianist or organist in a nickelodeon theater during frightening scenes in a film.

Twins (i): The premise is taken from Marie de France's *lai* "Le Fresne." In the story, a woman has given birth to twin girls. She is accused of adultery, as a woman who gave birth to two children at once was believed to have slept with two men.

Adulteress: The italicized text is from the French children's song "Alouette." Loosely translated, it reads, "Lark, you are a bloody torso."

The Resurrectionists: Epigraphs in quotations are taken from *The History of Burke and Hare and The Resurrectionist Times* by George Mac Gregor. In "J. J. Audubon on His Stay in Edinburgh," the italicized lines are taken from his letters. In "William Burke at His Dissection," the italicized lines are taken from his written confession.

Mirror Songs: The title of each poem in this section refers to which of John Berryman's Dream Songs it converses with.

Mesocyclone owes a debt to Alison Stine's "Again."

Autotheism: The final line is adapted from Ausonius.